In Memory of

Robert W. White

Presented by

His Family

What's it like to be a...
FIRE FIGHTER

Written by Michael J. Pellowski
Illustrated by John Lawn

Troll Associates

Special Consultant: Louis Cannizzaro, *Fire Chief, Palisades Park, New Jersey.*

Library of Congress Cataloging-in-Publication Data

Pellowski, Michael.
   Fire fighter / by Michael J. Pellowski; illustrated by John
Lawn.
     p.   cm.—(What's it like to be a...)
   Summary: Describes the many activities fire fighters perform in
their jobs and the various ways in which they put out fires.
   ISBN 0-8167-1428-2 (lib. bdg.)   ISBN 0-8167-1429-0 (pbk.)
   1. Fire fighters—Juvenile literature.   2. Fire extinction—
Juvenile literature. [1. Fire fighters. 2. Fire extinction.
3. Occupations.] I. Lawn, John, ill. II. Title. III. Series.
TH9148.P38   1989
628.9'2—dc19   88-10353

What's it like to be a...
FIRE FIGHTER

Fire!

It is useful. It is also dangerous. A fire out of control can hurt people and destroy property. It is the job of special people to put out fires. These people are fire fighters.

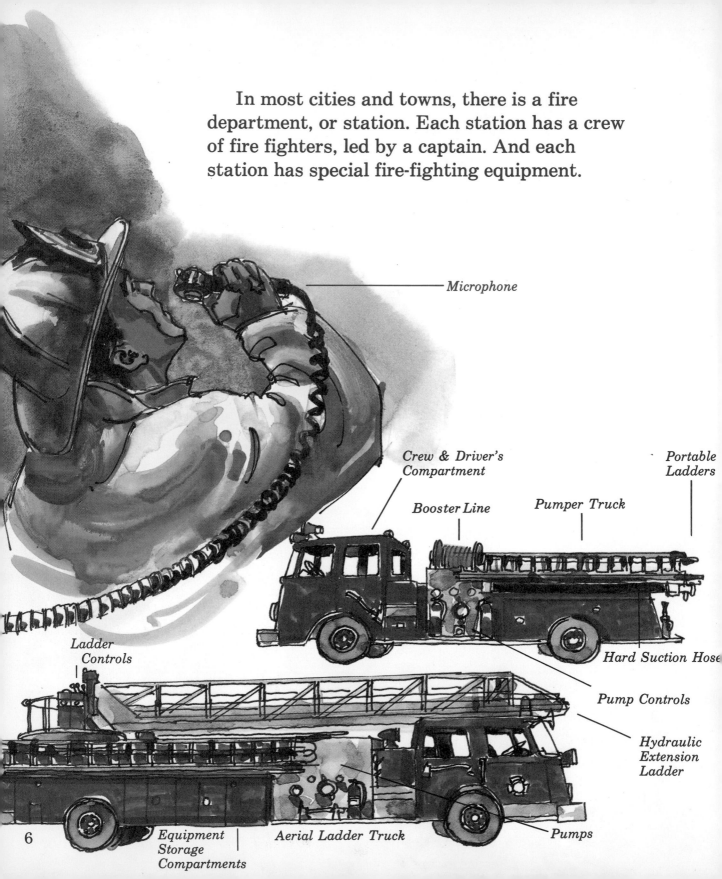

In most cities and towns, there is a fire department, or station. Each station has a crew of fire fighters, led by a captain. And each station has special fire-fighting equipment.

Microphone

Crew & Driver's Compartment

Portable Ladders

Booster Line

Pumper Truck

Ladder Controls

Hard Suction Hose

Pump Controls

Hydraulic Extension Ladder

Equipment Storage Compartments

Aerial Ladder Truck

Pumps

Rappelling

Training Tower

Bullhorn

Portable Ladder

Fire fighters are specially trained men and women. They go to a school where they learn to put out fires. Most important, they learn to work together as a team. They also are taught how to help people who've been hurt in a fire.

Pumper Truck

Rescue Truck

Fire fighters must know how to use many
kinds of equipment and fire trucks. Pumpers are
hose trucks. They pump water to put out a fire.
Rescue trucks help people hurt in fires and
accidents.

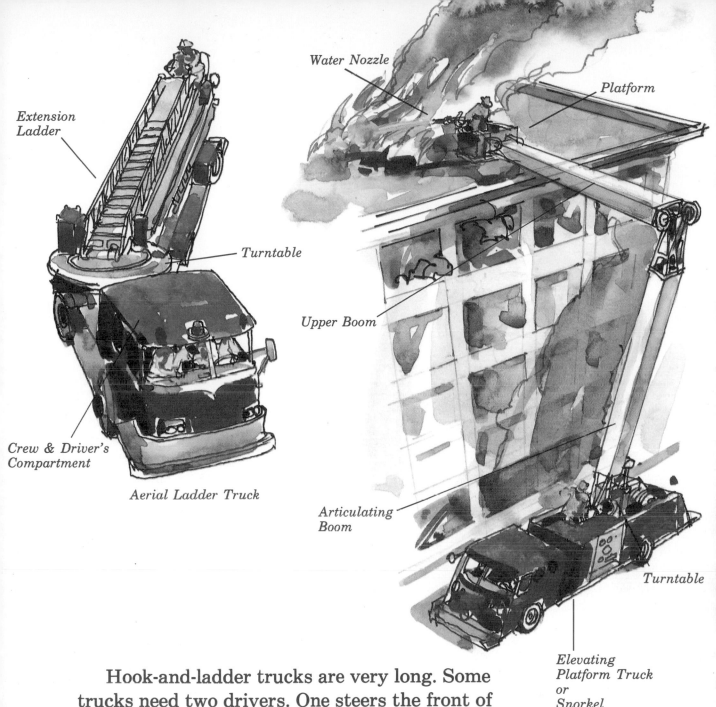

Extension
Ladder

Water Nozzle

Platform

Turntable

Upper Boom

Crew & Driver's
Compartment

Articulating
Boom

Aerial Ladder Truck

Turntable

Elevating
Platform Truck
or
Snorkel

Hook-and-ladder trucks are very long. Some trucks need two drivers. One steers the front of the truck. Another steers the back.

Big, city fire departments also use special fire-fighting equipment. Snorkel and water tower trucks shoot water high up into skyscrapers. Long aerial ladders stretch ten stories high.

Fire stations are busy places. Each fire crew takes a turn staying there for twenty-four hours. The crew must be ready to put out a fire at all times.

Fire Pole

Pumper Truck

Hard Suction Hoses

Pike Poles

Ax

Operating Lever

Hose

Hose Connection

Air Line

Flashing Lights

The crew eats and sleeps at the fire station. "What's for lunch?" asks a hungry fire fighter. He is shining a fire truck. Between fires, fire fighters work at the station. Every member of the crew helps.

Portable Ladder

Hand Holds

Equipment Storage Compartments

Hoses

Pressure Tank

Portable Fire Extinguisher

Crew members shine trucks, make beds, and sweep floors. They take turns food shopping, cooking, and washing dishes. It is like being part of a big family.

"Beef stew is for lunch," says the captain.
Today is his turn to cook.

13

BONG! BONG! BONG!
The alarm sounds! Lunch must wait. A fire
has been called into the fire department. Stations
nearest the fire are being alerted.

Fire Pole

The captain answers the call. He learns where the fire is.

"A factory's burning at Elm Street and Fourth Avenue," he shouts. "Let's move!"

Fire fighters rush to get ready. Some slide down the fire pole—the fastest way to get downstairs.

15

Quickly, the crew dresses in special fireproof clothes. On go boots, coats, gloves, and canvas pants. To protect their heads, the fire fighters wear special hard hats.

Hard Hat

Fire-Resistant Coat

Gloves

Canvas Pants

Boots

Hard Suction Hose

Pumper Truck

Booster Line

Portable Ladder

Hoses

Portable Fire Extinguishers

In seconds, the crew is ready to go. CLANK!
Up goes the station-house door.

The fire fighters climb aboard the truck.
DING! DING! WHIRRR! The siren blasts!
Away they go.

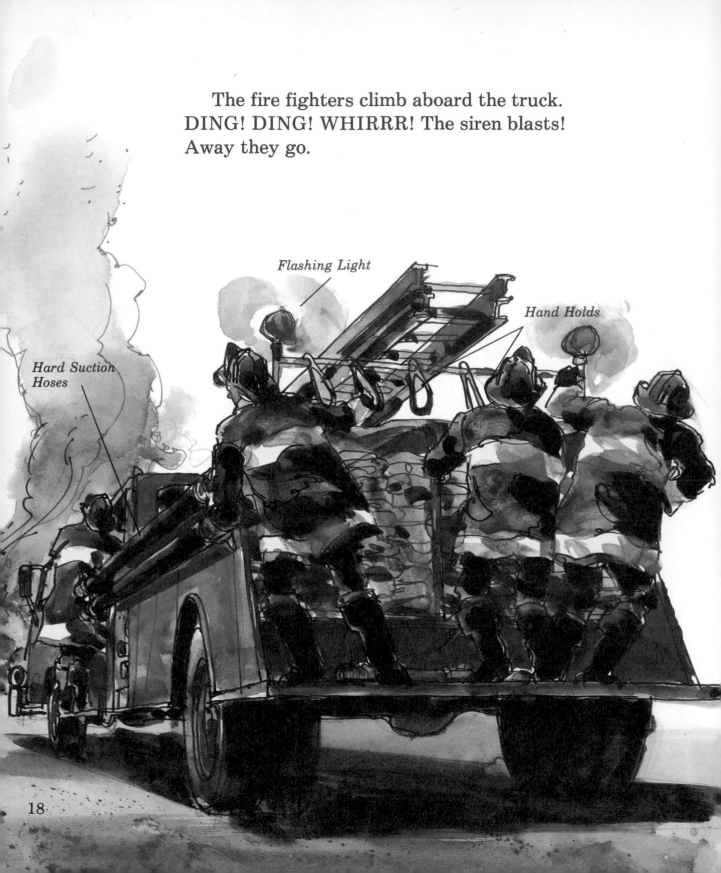

Flashing Light

Hand Holds

Hard Suction
Hoses

First at the fire are the pumper trucks. Fire fighters connect hoses to hydrants. The building must be wet down. WHOOSH! The pumper makes the water come out fast. It takes many fire fighters to hold the hose.

Water Nozzle

Hose

Control Valves

Air Cylinder

Face Mask

Air Line

Extension Ladder

Ax

Aerial Ladder Truck

Pike Pole

Hook-and-ladder trucks arrive next. The job of these fire fighters is to rescue people. Up go long ladders. Fire fighters put on masks so they will not breathe in the smoke. They take axes and special hooks from the truck.

The captain shouts an order, "Go!" Up the ladders climb the fire fighters. Modern fire trucks have hoses built into the extension ladder.

Turntable

Walkie-Talkie

Some chop holes in the roof to allow fire to escape. Others pry open windows. Brave fire fighters go into the burning building. They rescue the people inside.

Halligan Tool

Flashing Lights

Horns

Pumper Truck

Pump Compartment

Booster Line

Water Open-Shut Valve

Hard Suction Hoses

Hose Connection

Quick Connector

Fire Hydrant

Water is used to put out this fire. But water is not always used. Fire fighters know how to put out many kinds of fires.

A special dry powder is used to put out motor fires. Fire needs air to burn. The powder smothers the flames. Foam is used on gas or oil fires. Sometimes fire fighters use water mixed with chemicals.

Nozzle

Chemical Powder

Operating Lever

Dry Chemical Extinguisher

Face Shield

Heat-Reflective Suit

Nozzle

Foam

Release Valve

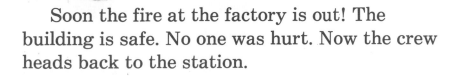

Soon the fire at the factory is out! The
building is safe. No one was hurt. Now the crew
heads back to the station.

Water Gun

Platform

Spotlight

Diesel-Powered Pump

Water
Guns

Not all fire fighters work at fire stations.
There are many kinds of fire fighters. Some work
on fire boats. Fire boats are used to put out fires
on ships. They also fight fires on the waterfront.

Rotor Blades

Turbine Exhaust

Helicopter

Tail Rotor

Landing
Gear

Float For
Water Landing

Chemical
Powder

Some fire fighters are pilots. They fly
airplanes and helicopters. They fight field, brush,
and forest fires. Pilots drop a special powder on
the fire below. The powder smothers the flames.

Smoke jumpers fight fire in a special way.
They fight forest fires that cannot be reached by
fire trucks. They travel in airplanes.

Safety Helmet

Main Parachute Pack

Fire-Retardant Jump Suit

Automatic
Release
Line

Emergency
Reserve Chute

Harness

28

Canopy

Suspension
Lines

Face
Mask

Riser

Steering
Line

Spade

Using parachutes, they jump from the planes.
With them, they carry their fire-fighting
equipment. The parachutes drop them to earth
near the blaze. Quickly, the smoke jumpers go
into action.

29

Portable
Fire
Extinguisher

Landing Marker

Sometimes smoke jumpers battle forest fires
for weeks. Airplanes drop supplies to the fire
fighters by parachute. When the fire is out, the
smoke jumpers hike back to camp.

Some fire fighters stop fires before they start.
These people are called fire inspectors.

"Everything is safe," says an inspector, after
checking a new building. "There are no fire
hazards here."

Smoke Detector

Fire Exit

EXIT

Safety Glass

Fire Safety
Door

Release
Bar

Air
Pressure
Gauge

Hose

Operating
Lever

Inspection
Tag

Pressure
Tank

Nozzle

Some towns have very well-trained volunteer fire fighters. They give their free time to fight fires. Whether in cities or small towns, whether in forests or at sea—brave fire fighters are always ready to do their job.

You, too, can be a fire fighter. How? Be careful with fire!